TULSA CITY-COUNTY LIBRARY

D0561071

JAN - - 2023

Dear Parent:

Your child's love of reading starts here!

Every child learns to read in a different way and at his or her own speed. Some go back and forth between reading levels and read favorite books again and again. Others read through each level in order. You can help your young reader improve and become more confident by encouraging his or her own interests and abilities. From books your child reads with you to the first books he or she reads alone, there are I Can Read Books for every stage of reading:

SHARED READING
Basic language, word repetition, and whimsical illustrations, ideal for sharing with your emergent reader

BEGINNING READING
Short sentences, familiar words, and simple concepts for children eager to read on their own

READING WITH HELP
Engaging stories, longer sentences, and language play for developing readers

READING ALONE
Complex plots, challenging vocabulary, and high-interest topics for the independent reader

I Can Read Books have introduced children to the joy of reading since 1957. Featuring award-winning authors and illustrators and a fabulous cast of beloved characters, I Can Read Books set the standard for beginning readers.

A lifetime of discovery begins with the magical words "I Can Read!"

Visit www.icanread.com for information
on enriching your child's reading experience.

1 BEGINNING READING · I Can Read!

Pinkalicious
and the Holiday Sweater

To Ellie and Emmy
—V.K.

The author gratefully acknowledges
the artistic and editorial contributions of
Daniel Griffo and Jacqueline Resnick.

I Can Read® and I Can Read Book® are trademarks of HarperCollins Publishers.

Pinkalicious and the Holiday Sweater
Copyright © 2022 by VBK, Co.

PINKALICIOUS and all related logos and characters are trademarks of VBK, Co. Used with permission.

Based on the HarperCollins book *Pinkalicious* written by
Victoria Kann and Elizabeth Kann, illustrated by Victoria Kann

All rights reserved. Printed in the United States of America.
No part of this book may be used or reproduced in any manner whatsoever without
written permission except in the case of brief quotations embodied in critical articles and reviews.
For information address HarperCollins Children's Books, a division of HarperCollins Publishers,
195 Broadway, New York, NY 10007.
www.icanread.com

Library of Congress Control Number: 2022935800
ISBN 978-0-06-300388-0 (trade bdg.)—ISBN 978-0-06-300387-3 (pbk.)

22 23 24 25 26 LSCC 10 9 8 7 6 5 4 3 2 1
❖
First Edition

Pinkalicious
and the Holiday Sweater

by Victoria Kann

HARPER
An Imprint of HarperCollinsPublishers

"Class, we are going to do a Secret Snowman gift exchange for the holidays this year!" said my teacher, Ms. Penny.

"What's a Secret Snowman?" I asked.

"You draw a name and make a gift
for the person you picked,"
Ms. Penny said.

"Everyone will say who they got
when we exchange the gifts
at our class holiday party."

"I wonder who I'll get!" I said.

I pulled out a name.

It was Molly!

"Who did you pick?" Molly asked.

"You'll have to wait and see,"

I said.

"Who did you get?" I asked.

"I can't tell you,"

she said mysteriously.

All morning,

I thought of gifts for Molly,

but none was good enough.

I wanted Molly's gift

to be as pinkamazing as she was!

I was still stumped
by lunchtime.
Then I heard Molly shout,
"OH NO!"

Molly had gotten ketchup

on her sweater!

"My favorite sweater is ruined!"

Molly said.

Suddenly I knew exactly

what to make for Molly.

"Can I have some yarn?"
I asked Mommy that night.
"I'm going to knit a sweater
for Molly's Secret Snowman gift!"

"A sweater is hard to knit,"

Mommy said.

"I've made hats and scarves before,"

I said.

"I'm sure I can make a sweater!"

I began to knit.

"Oops," I said, as I yanked my yarn.

"Oops," I said,

as my stitches snagged.

I worked all week.

I ran out of yarn,

but I didn't give up.

I found an extra ball of yarn

and kept knitting.

Finally, I was done!

"Ta-da!" I said to Mommy and Peter.

I held up my sweater.

"Presenting the most

pinkamazing, pinkadazzling . . ."

I trailed off.

Then I looked at my sweater.

The bottom was uneven,

one arm was too long,

and it had a lot of holes.

"My sweater is a mess!" I said.

"I like the colors," Peter said.

"Molly will like it because

you made it for her," Mommy said.

I shook my head.

"I can't give this to Molly,"

I said sadly.

"Now I don't have a gift

for tomorrow's Secret Snowman!"

"I'm looking for Pinkalicious!"

Daddy said as he came into the room.

"I need fashion advice.

Do you think my sweater is ugly?"

"Well . . ." I said with a laugh.

"Perfect!" Daddy said.

"We're having an ugly

holiday sweater party at work."

"It just needs one more thing,"

Peter said.

He draped Daddy with garland.

"Peter, you're a genius!" I gasped.

"I know," Peter said.

"But . . . why?"

I didn't have time to answer.

I had work to do!

I gathered my supplies.

I knitted. I sewed.

I glued.

In school the next day, I was ready.

"Happy holidays!" said Ms. Penny.

"It's time for our Secret Snowman."

I opened my gift.

I got a pink tiara . . .

made by Molly!

"Now you know who I got,"

Molly said with a laugh.

I gave Molly my gift.

"I picked you!" I said.

Molly unwrapped my gift.

"It's a holiday sweater!

I've always wanted one!" Molly said.

Molly put on the sweater

and did a spin.

The sweater shined and shimmered.

"You twinkle when you twirl!"

I said.

"I want to make a
holiday sweater!" Alison said.

"I want a knitted holiday hat,"
Jack said.

"Maybe Pinkalicious can give us
all a lesson," Ms. Penny suggested.

Ms. Penny brought needles and yarn
to school the next day.
I taught my class how to knit!

"Don't forget to add your holiday decorations!" I said. "'Tis the season to make everything sparklerrific!"